BILLY JOEL FOR UKULELE

ISBN 978-1-4803-5353-4

HAL•LEONARD® CORPORATION

7777 W. BLUEMOUND RD. P.O. BOX 13819 MILWAUKEE, WI 53213

In Australia Contact:
Hal Leonard Australia Pty. Ltd.
4 Lentara Court
Cheltenham, Victoria, 3192 Australia
Email: ausadmin@halleonard.com.au

Visit Hal Leonard Online at
www.halleonard.com

CONTENTS

And So It Goes

Words and Music by Billy Joel

The Entertainer

Words and Music by Billy Joel

oth - er year ___ if I don't stay on the charts. ___

2. I

G ... C ... Dm

am the en - ter - tain - er and I've had to pay ___ my

3.–7. See additional lyrics

C ... G

price. The things I did ___ not know ___ at first, ___ I

C ... D ... G

learned by do - ing twice. ___ But still they come to haunt ___

C ... Dm ... C

___ me; still they want ___ their say. So I've

D ... Am7

learned to dance ___ with a hand in my pants. Let 'em rub my neck ___ and I

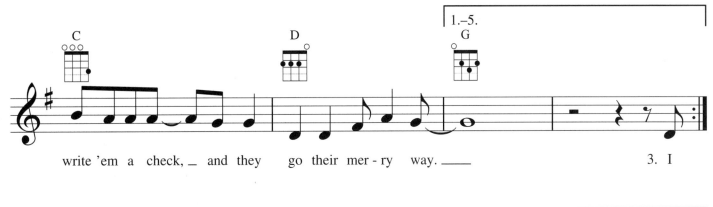

write 'em a   check, __ and they   go their mer - ry   way. _____   3. I

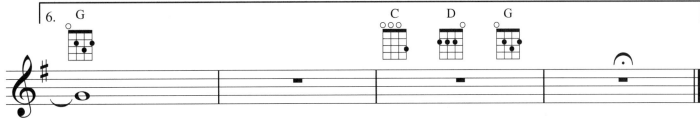

Additional Lyrics

3. I am the entertainer, been all around the world,
   I've played all kinds of palaces and laid all kinds of girls.
   I can't remember faces; I don't remember names.
   But what the hell, you know it's just as well
   'Cause after a while and a thousand miles
   It all becomes the same.

4. I am the entertainer; I bring to you my songs.
   I'd like to spend a day or two but I can't stay that long.
   I got to meet expenses; I got to stay in line.
   Got to get those fees to the agencies
   And I'd love to stay, but there's bills to pay
   So I just don't have the time.

5. I am the entertainer; I've come to do my show.
   You've heard my latest record; it's been on the radio.
   It took me years to write it; they were the best years of my life.
   It was a beautiful song, but it ran too long.
   If you're gonna have a hit, you gotta make it fit
   So they cut it down to 3:05.

6. I am the entertainer, the idol of my age.
   I make all kinds of money when I go on the stage.
   You've seen me in the papers; I've been in the magazines.
   But if I go cold, I won't get sold.
   I get put in the back in the discount rack
   Like another can of beans.

7. I am the entertainer and I know just where I stand,
   Another serenader and another long-haired band.
   Today I am your champion; I may have won your hearts.
   But I know the game; you'll forget my name.
   I won't be here in another year
   If I don't stay on the charts.

Don't Ask Me Why

Words and Music by Billy Joel

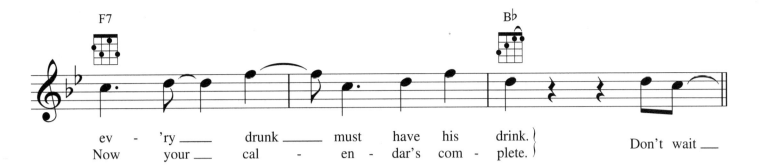

ev - 'ry _____ drunk _____ must have his drink.
Now your _____ cal - en - dar's com - plete. Don't wait _____

_____ for an - swers; just take _____ your chanc -

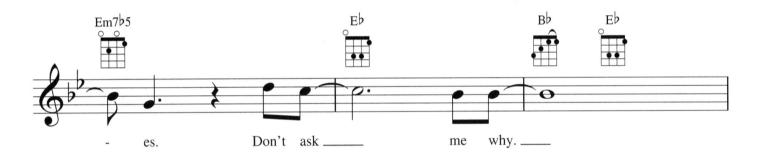

- es. Don't ask _____ me why. _____

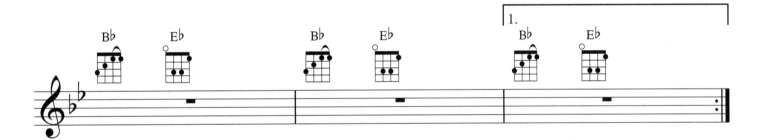

1.

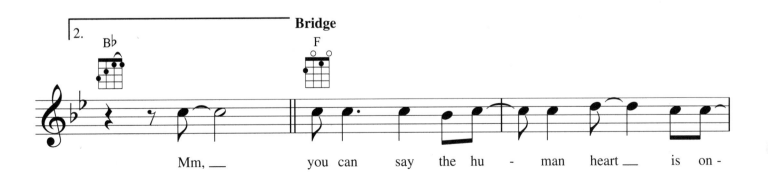

2. **Bridge**

Mm, _____ you can say the hu - man heart _____ is on -

-ly make be - lieve, ___ and I am on - ly

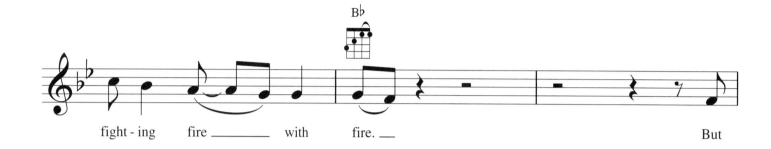

fight - ing fire _____ with fire. ___ But

you are still a vic - tim of the ac - ci - dents ___ you leave, ___

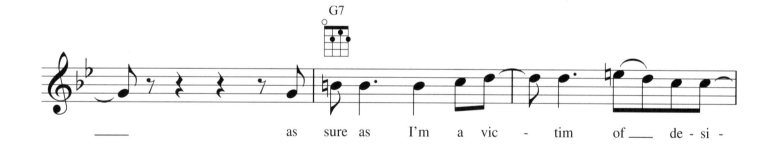

_____ as sure as I'm a vic - tim of ___ de - si -

- yi - yi - re. 3. All the ___ ser -
4. Yes - ter - day ___

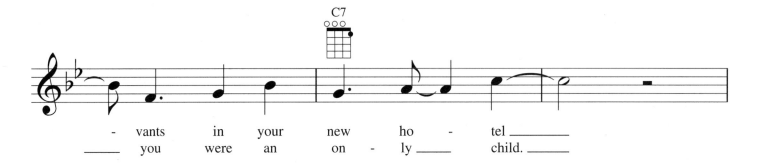

- vants in your new ho - tel _____
_____ you were an on - ly _____ child. _____

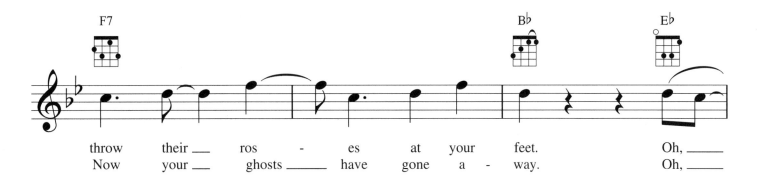

throw their _____ ros - es at your feet. Oh, _____
Now your _____ ghosts _____ have gone a - way. Oh, _____

_____ fool them _____ all, _____ but, ba - by,
_____ you can _____ kill _____ them in the

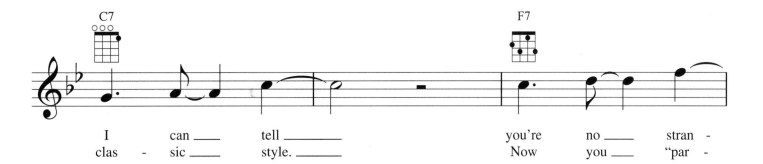

I can _____ tell _____ you're no _____ stran -
clas - sic _____ style. _____ Now you _____ "par -

Chorus

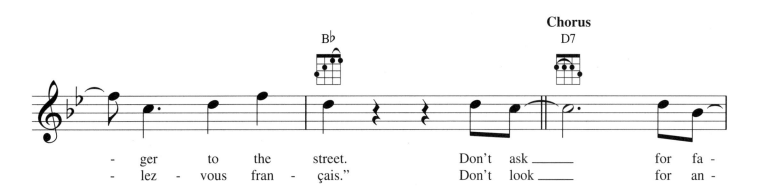

- ger to the street. Don't ask _____ for fa -
- lez - vous fran - çais." Don't look _____ for an -

13

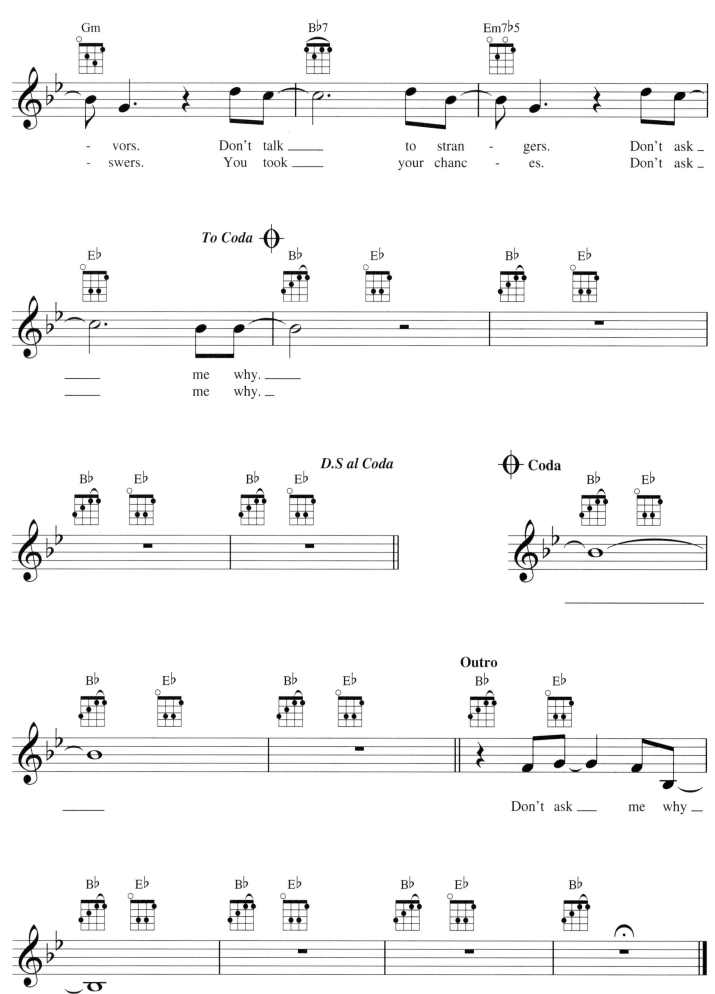

It's Still Rock and Roll to Me

Words and Music by Billy Joel

First note

Verse
Moderately fast Rock Shuffle

1. What's the mat- ter with the clothes I'm wear- in'? "Can't you
2.–4. *See additional lyrics*

tell that your tie's too wide?" ___ May- be I should buy some

old tab col- lars. "Wel- come back to the age of jive. _____

Where have you been hid- in' out late- ly, hon- ey? You

can't dress trash- y 'til you spend a lot of mon- ey."

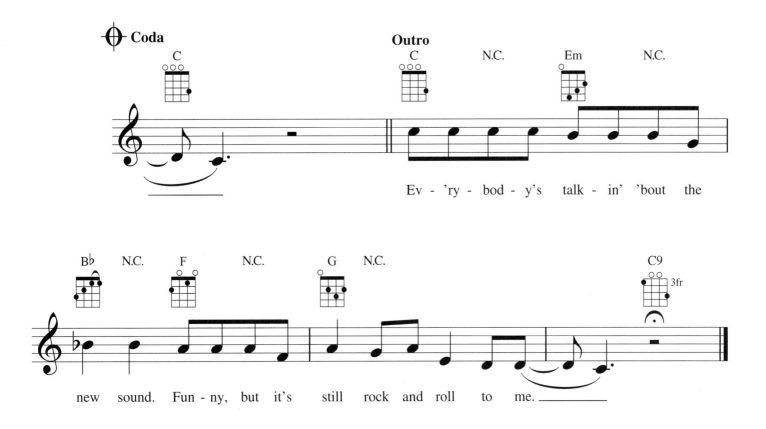

Ev - 'ry - bod - y's talk - in' 'bout the new sound. Fun - ny, but it's still rock and roll to me. _____

Additional Lyrics

2. What's the matter with the car I'm drivin'?
   "Can't you tell that it's out of style?"
   Should I get a set of whitewall tires?
   "Are you gonna cruise the miracle mile?
   Nowadays you can't be too sentimental.
   Your best bet's a true baby blue Continental."
   Hot funk, cool punk, even if it's old junk,
   It's still rock and roll to me.

3. How about a pair of pink side-winders
   And a bright orange pair of pants?
   "Well, you could really be a Beau Brummell, baby,
   If you just give it half a chance.
   Don't waste your money on a new set of speakers.
   You get more mileage from a cheap pair of sneakers."
   Next phase, new wave dance craze, anyways,
   It's still rock and roll to me.

4. What's the matter with the crowd I'm seein'?
   "Don't you know that they're out of touch?"
   Well, should I try to be a straight "A" student?
   "If you are, then you think too much.
   Don't you know about the new fashion, honey?
   All you need are looks and a whole lot of money."
   It's the next phase, new wave dance craze, anyways,
   It's still rock and roll to me.

Honesty

Words and Music by Billy Joel

Ev - 'ry - one is so un - true. ____

Hon - es - ty ____ is hard - ly ev - er heard, ____ but

To Coda

1.

2.

most - ly what I need from you. ____

Bridge

I can find a lov - er,

I can find a friend, __ I can have se - cur - i - ty ____ un -

til the bit - ter end. ____ An - y - one can com - fort me ____ with

prom - is - es _____ a - gain, _____ I know, _____ I

Verse

know. _____ 3. When I'm _____ deep in - side of me _____

don't be too con - cerned. _____ I won't _____ ask for noth - in' while I'm

gone. When I _____ want sin - cer - i - ty, tell me, where _____

_____ else can I turn? _____ 'Cause you're the one _____ that I _____ de - pend up - on. _____

D.S. al Coda

Coda

My Life

Words and Music by Billy Joel

Now he gives _ them a stand - up rou - tine _ in L. A. _
Go a - head _ with your own _ life; _ leave _ me a - lone. _
Ei - ther way, _ it's o - kay; _ you wake up _ with your - self. _

1., 3.

2., 4.

Bridge

_ I nev - er said you had to of - fer me a sec - ond chance. _

I nev - er said I was a vic - tim of cir -

- cum - stance. _ I still be - long. _

_ Don't get me wrong. _ You _ can speak _

Just the Way You Are

Words and Music by Billy Joel

First note

Verse
Moderately, in 2

1. Don't go chang - ing _____ to try and please _____
2. Don't go try - ing _____ some new fash -

_____ me; you nev - er let me down _____ be - fore. _____
- ion; don't change the col - or of _____ your hair. _____

_____ Mm. _____ Don't i - mag -
_____ Mm. _____ You al - ways have _____

- ine you're too fa - mil - iar
_____ my un - spo - ken pas - sion,

and I don't see _____ you an - y - more. _____
al - though I might _____ not _____ seem to care. _____

Leave a Tender Moment Alone

Words and Music by Billy Joel

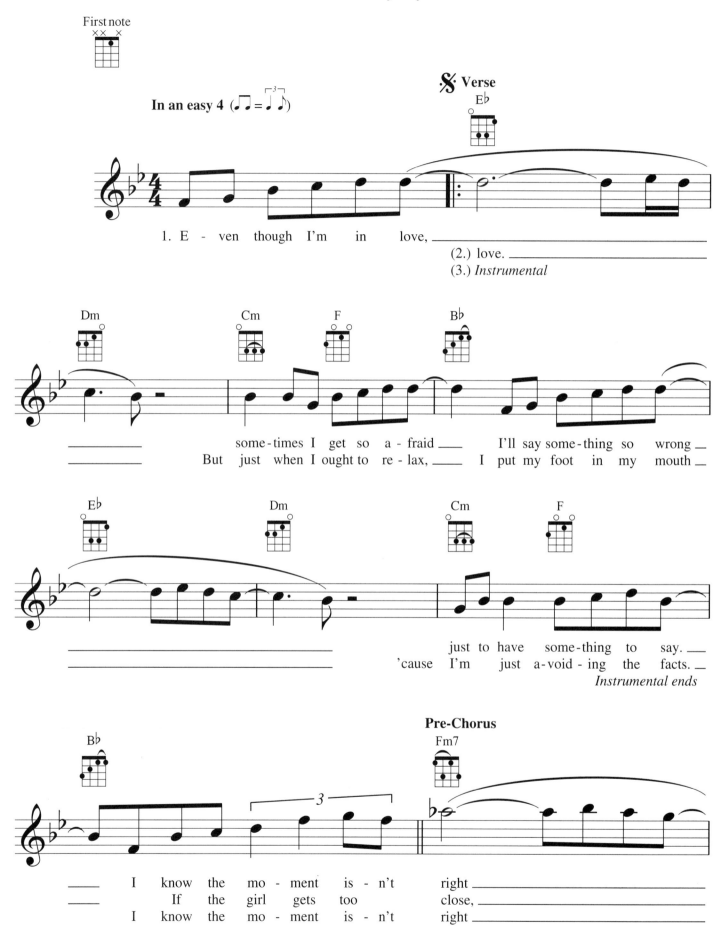

to tell the girl a com - i - cal line ____ to keep the con - ver - sa - tion
if I ____ need some room to es - cape ____ when the mo - ment a -
to hold ___ my e - mo - tions in - side, ____ to change the at - ti - tude to -

light. _____ I guess I'm just fright - ened out of my mind. __
rose, _____ I'd tell her it's all a mis - take. __
night. _____ I've run out of plac - es to hide. __

Chorus

____ But if that's how I feel, _____ then it's the
____ But that's not how I feel. _____ No,
____ And if that's how I feel, _____ then it's the

best feel - ing I've ev - er known. __ It's un - de - ni - a - bly real. _____
that's not the wom - an I've known. __ She's un - de - ni - a - bly real. _____
best feel - ing I've ev - er known. __ It's un - de - ni - a - bly real. _____

To Coda

____ Leave a ten - der mo - ment a - lone. ____ 2. Yes, I know I'm in
____ So leave a ten - der mo - ment a - lone. __
____ Leave a ten - der mo - ment a - lone. __

But it's not on - ly me _____ break-ing down ___ when the ten -

- sion gets high. ___ Just when I'm _____ in a se - ri - ous mood, ___

she is sud - den - ly qui - et and shy. ___ *Instrumental*

D.S. al Coda

⊕ Coda

Outro

Leave a ten - der mo - ment a - lone. ___

Leave a ten - der mo - ment a - lone. ___

Only the Good Die Young

Words and Music by Billy Joel

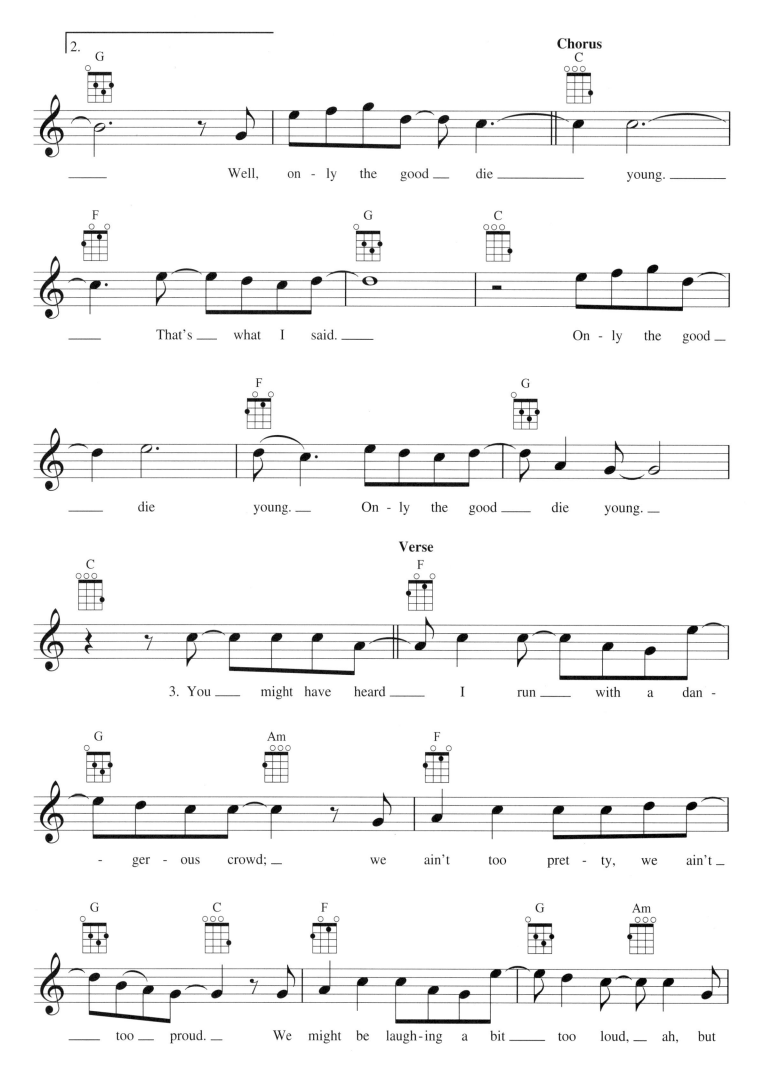

Chorus

Well, on - ly the good __ die __ young. __

That's __ what I said. __ On - ly the good __

__ die young. __ On - ly the good __ die young. __

Verse

3. You __ might have heard __ I run __ with a dan -

- ger - ous crowd; __ we ain't too pret - ty, we ain't __

__ too __ proud. __ We might be laugh-ing a bit __ too loud, __ ah, but

that nev-er hurt ___ no one. ___   4. So come on, _____   Vir - gin - ia,   show ___
___ there's a heav - en   for those ___

_____ me   a   sign. ___   Send   up   a   sig - nal;   I'll
_____ who   will   wait. ___   Some   say   it's   bet - ter,   but   I ___

throw   you   a   line. ___   That   stained - glass   cur - tain   you're   hid -
___ say   it   ain't. ___   I'd   rath - er   laugh   with   the   sin - ners   than   cry ___

- ing   be - hind ___   nev - er   lets   in   the   sun. ___
_____ with   the   saints; ___   the   sin - ners   are   much   more   fun. ___

Chorus

_____   Dar - lin',   on - ly   the   good ___ die _____   young. _____
_____   You   know   that   on - ly   the   good ___ die _____   young. _____

_____   Whoa, _____   on - ly   the   good ___ die
_____   That's   what   I   say.   On - ly   the   good ___ die

young. __ On - ly the good __ die young. __ You got a
young. __ On - ly the good __ die young. __ *Instrumental*

Bridge

nice white dress and a par - ty on your con - fir - ma -

- tion. _____ You've __ got a brand - new soul _____

_____ and a cross __ of __ gold. _____ But, Vir -
End instrumental Said your

gin - ia, they did - n't give you quite e - nough in - for - ma -
moth - er told you all that I could give you was a rep - u - ta -

- tion. _____ You __ did - n't count __ on me _____
- tion. _____ She nev - er cared for me. _____

The Longest Time

Words and Music by Billy Joel

What else could I do? I'm so in-spired _ by you.
That's where you found me when you put your arms a-round me.

That has-n't hap-pened for the long-est time.
I have-n't been there for the long-est time.

Chorus

Oh, oh, oh, oh. For the long-est

time. Oh, oh, oh. For the long-est...

Verse

3. I'm that voice you're hear-ing in the hall.
4. Who knows how much fur-ther we'll go on?

And the great-est mir-a-cle of all
May-be I'll be sor-ry when you're gone.

Chord diagrams: G7, Cm, B♭7, E♭, E♭7

is how I need you and how you need - ed me too.
I'll take my chanc - es; I for - got how nice ro - mance is.

Chord diagrams: A♭ (3fr), Fm, B♭, E♭

That has - n't hap - pened for the long - est time.
I have - n't been there for the long - est time.

Bridge

Chord diagrams: B♭, Cm

May - be this won't last ver - y long, but
I had sec - ond thoughts at the start. I

Chord diagrams: D7, E♭

you feel so right, and I could be wrong.
said to my - self and hold on to your heart.

Chord diagrams: Gm, Cm

May - be I've been hop - ing too hard, but
Now I know the wom - an that you are. You're

Chord diagrams: F, F7, B♭, B♭7

I've gone this far and it's more than I hoped for.
won - der - ful so far, and it's more than I hoped for.

Lullabye
(Goodnight, My Angel)

Words and Music by Billy Joel

I nev-er will be far a-way.

you'll al-ways be a part of me.

Verse

3. Good-night, my an-gel, now it's time to dream, and dream how won-der-ful your

life will be. Some-day your child may cry, and if you sing this lull-a-bye,

then in your heart there will al-ways be a part of me.

Outro

Some-day we'll all be gone, but lull-a-byes go on and on.

They nev-er die; that's how you and __ I will be.

New York State of Mind

Words and Music by Billy Joel

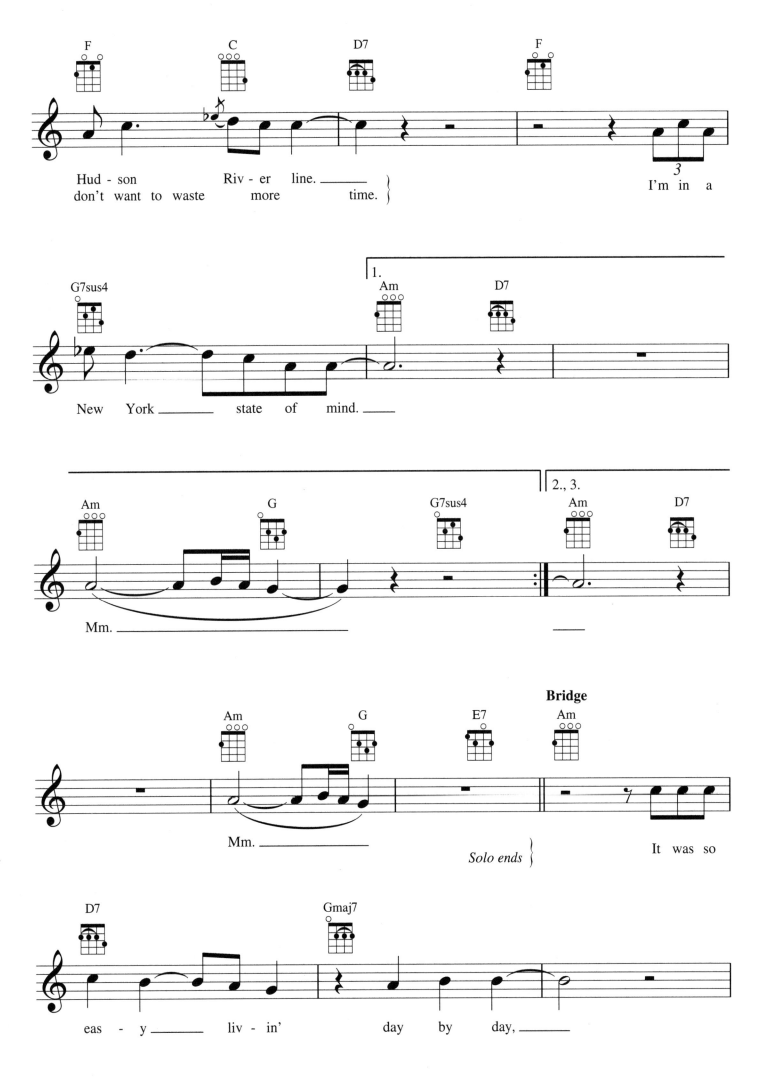

out of touch with the rhy-thm and blues.

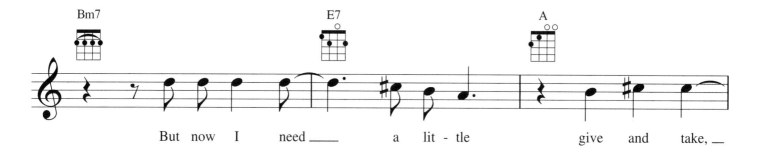

But now I need — a lit-tle give and take, —

— the New York Times, —— the

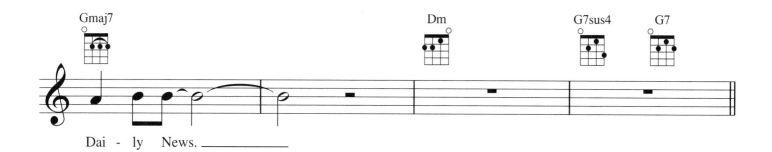

Dai - ly News. ——

Verse

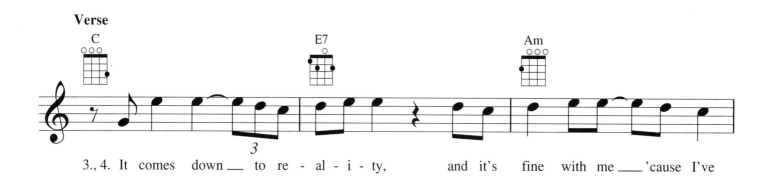

3., 4. It comes down — to re - al - i - ty, and it's fine with me — 'cause I've

To Coda ⊕

D.C. al Coda
(take 2nd ending)

⊕ **Coda**

Piano Man

Words and Music by Billy Joel

F   G7sus4   C

love   to   his   ton - ic   and   gin.
some - place   that   he'd   rath - er   be.
prob - ab - ly   will   be   for   life.
get   a - bout   life   for   a   while.

F   G   G7sus4

He   says,
He   says,
And   the
And   the

C   G   Am

"Son,   can   you   play   me   a   mem - o - ry?
"Bill,   I   be - lieve   this   is   kill - ing   me,"
wait - ress   is   prac - tic - ing   pol - i - tics,
pia - no   sounds   like   a   car - ni - val,

C   F   C

I'm   not   real - ly   sure   how   it
as   a   smile   ran   a - way   from   his
as   the   bus' - ness - men   slow - ly   get
and   the   mic - ro - phone   smells   like   a

D7   G   C

goes.   But   it's   sad   and   it's
face.   "Well,   I'm   sure   that   I
stoned.   Yes,   they're   shar - ing   a
beer.   And   they   sit   at   the

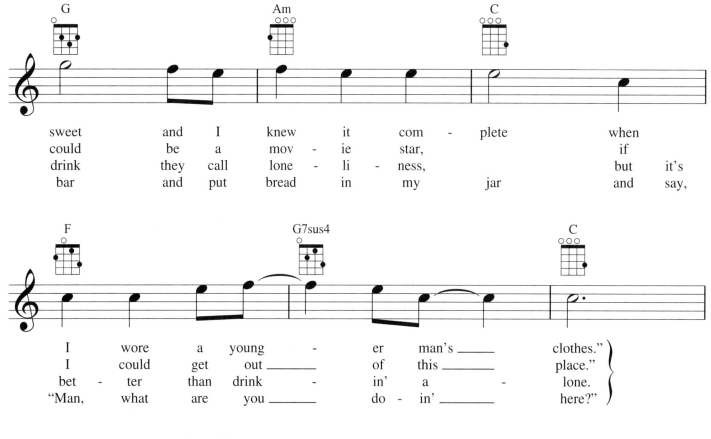

sweet · · and I knew it com - plete · · when
could · · be a mov - ie star, · · · if
drink · · they call lone - li - ness, · · but it's
bar · · and put bread in my jar · · and say,

I wore a young - er man's _____ clothes." 〉
I could get out _____ of this _____ place." 〉
bet - ter than drink - in' a - lone. 〉
"Man, what are you _____ do - in' _____ here?" 〉

Pre-Chorus

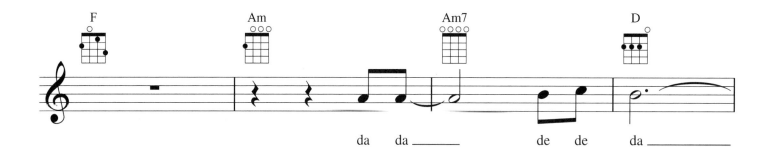

Da da da _____ de de da, _____

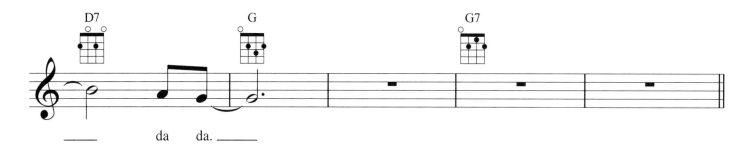

da da _____ de de da _____

_____ da da. _____

48

Chorus

Sing us a song, _____ you're the pia - no man. _____

Sing us a song _____ to - night. _____

Well, we're all in the mood _____ for a mel - o - dy,

and you've got us feel - in' al - right.

1.–3.   4.

2. Now,
3. Now,
4. It's a

The River of Dreams

Words and Music by Billy Joel

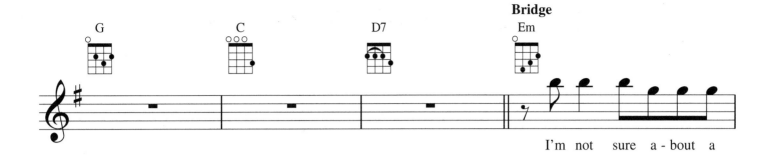

Bridge

I'm not sure a-bout a

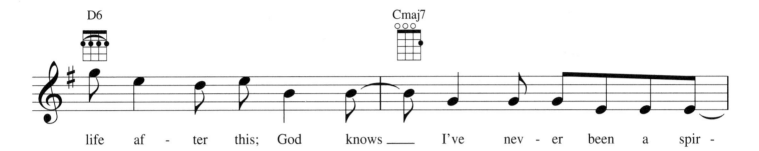

life af - ter this; God knows ___ I've nev - er been a spir -

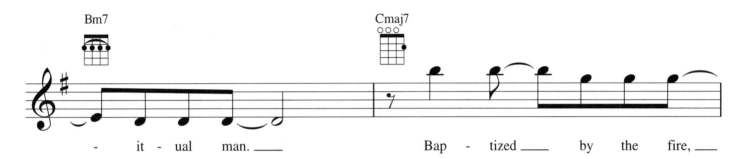

- it - ual man. ___ Bap - tized ___ by the fire, ___

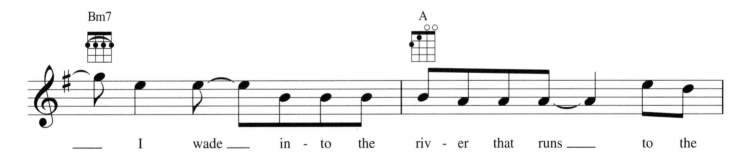

___ I wade ___ in - to the riv - er that runs ___ to the

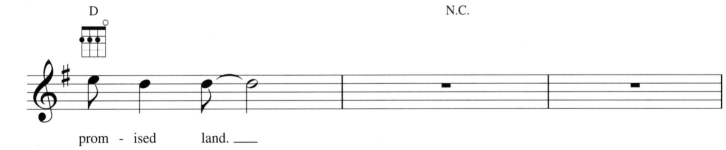

prom - ised land. ___

D.S. al Coda

Coda

4. In the mid - dle of the

night. ___

She's Always a Woman

Words and Music by Billy Joel

time. _____ Oh, _____ and she nev - er gives

out, _____ and she nev - er gives in. She just chang - es her

Verse

mind. 3. And she'll prom - ise you more than the gar - den of
4. She is fre - quent - ly kind and she's sud - den - ly

E - den, then she'll care - less - ly cut you and laugh while you're
cru - el. She can do as she pleas - es; she's no - bod - y's

To Coda ⊕

bleed - in'. But she brings out the best and the worst you can be. Blame it
fool. ___ But she can't be con - vict - ed; she's earned her de - gree. And the

all on your-self 'cause she's al-ways a wom-an to me. *(Hum)*

Interlude

D.S. al Coda

Coda

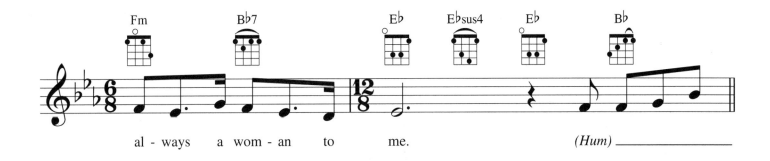

most she will do is throw shad-ows at you, but she's

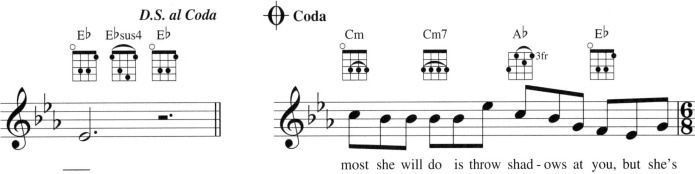

al - ways a wom-an to me. *(Hum)*

Outro

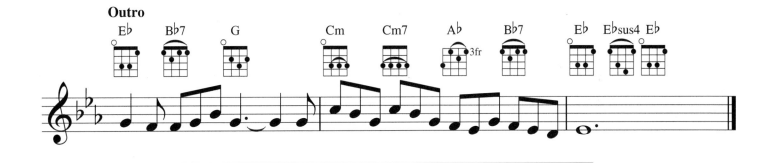

She's Got a Way

Words and Music by Billy Joel

Bridge

She comes to me ___ when I'm feel-in' down, ___ in-

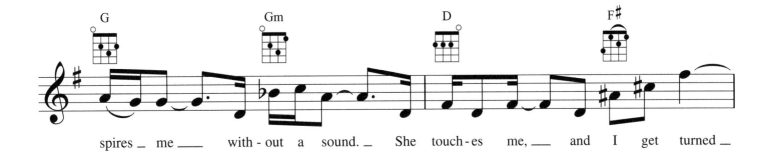

spires ___ me ___ with-out a sound. ___ She touch-es me, ___ and I get turned ___

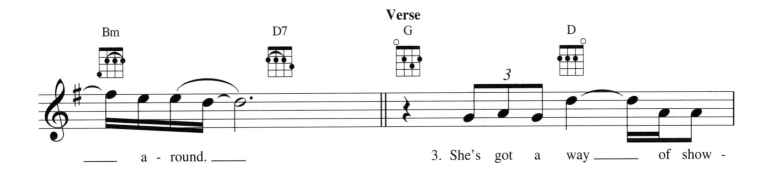

Verse

___ a - round. ___ 3. She's got a way ___ of show -

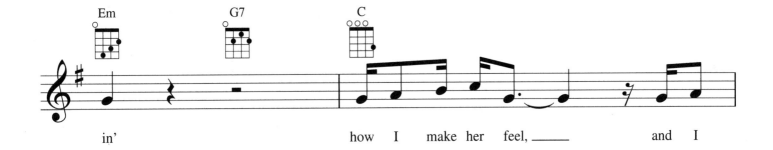

in' how I make her feel, ___ and I

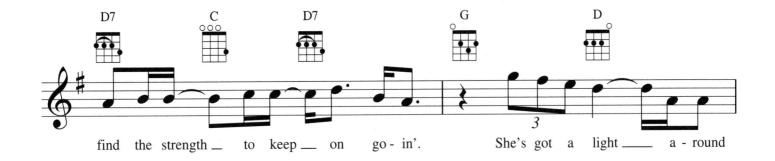

find the strength ___ to keep ___ on go-in'. She's got a light ___ a-round

Tell Her About It

Words and Music by Billy Joel

You May Be Right

Words and Music by Billy Joel

First note

Verse
Moderate Rock

1. Fri - day night __ I crashed __ your par - ty.
(2.) - ed in __ the com - bat zone. __ I
(3.) - ber how __ I found __ you there __ a -
(4.) __ of all __ the years __ you tried __ to

Sat - ur - day __ I said __ I'm sor - ry.
walked through Bed - ford Stuy __ a - lone, __ e - ven rode __
lone in your __ e - lec - tric chair; __ I told __
find some - one __ to sat - is - fy __ you.

Sun - day came __ and trashed __ me out __ a - gain. __
__ my mo - tor - cy - cle in __ the rain. __
__ you dirt - y jokes __ un - til __ you smiled. __
I might be __ as cra - zy as __ you say. __

I was on - ly hav - ing fun, __
And you told __ me not __ to drive, __
You were lone - ly for __ a man. __
If I'm cra - zy, then __ it's true __

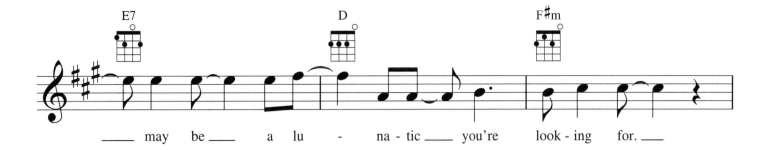

_____ may be ____ a lu - na - tic ____ you're look-ing for. _____

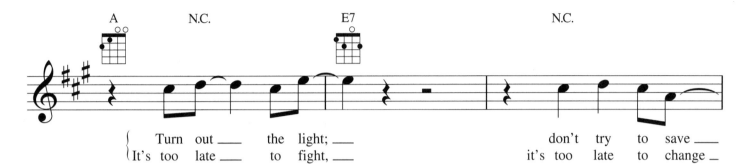

{ Turn out ____ the light; ____   don't try to save ____
{ It's too late ____ to fight, ____   it's too late to change __

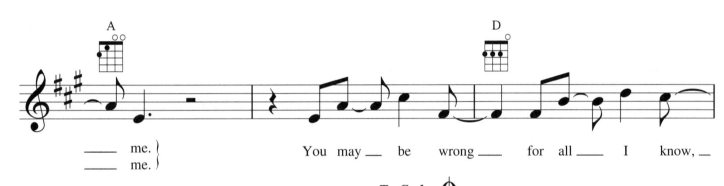

____ me. }   You may ___ be wrong ___ for all ___ I know, __
____ me. }

To Coda

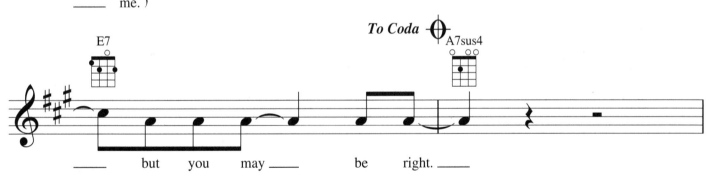

____ but you may ____ be right. _____

Coda

D.C. al Coda
(with repeat)

3. Well, re - mem -

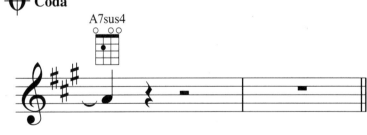

_____

Outro

**Repeat ad lib. and fade**

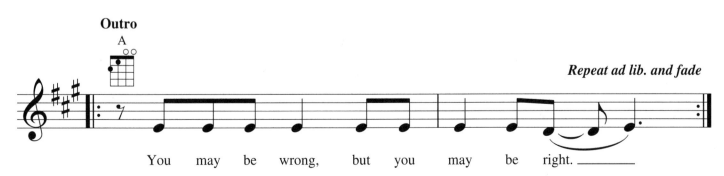

You may be wrong, but you may be right. _____

Uptown Girl

Words and Music by Billy Joel

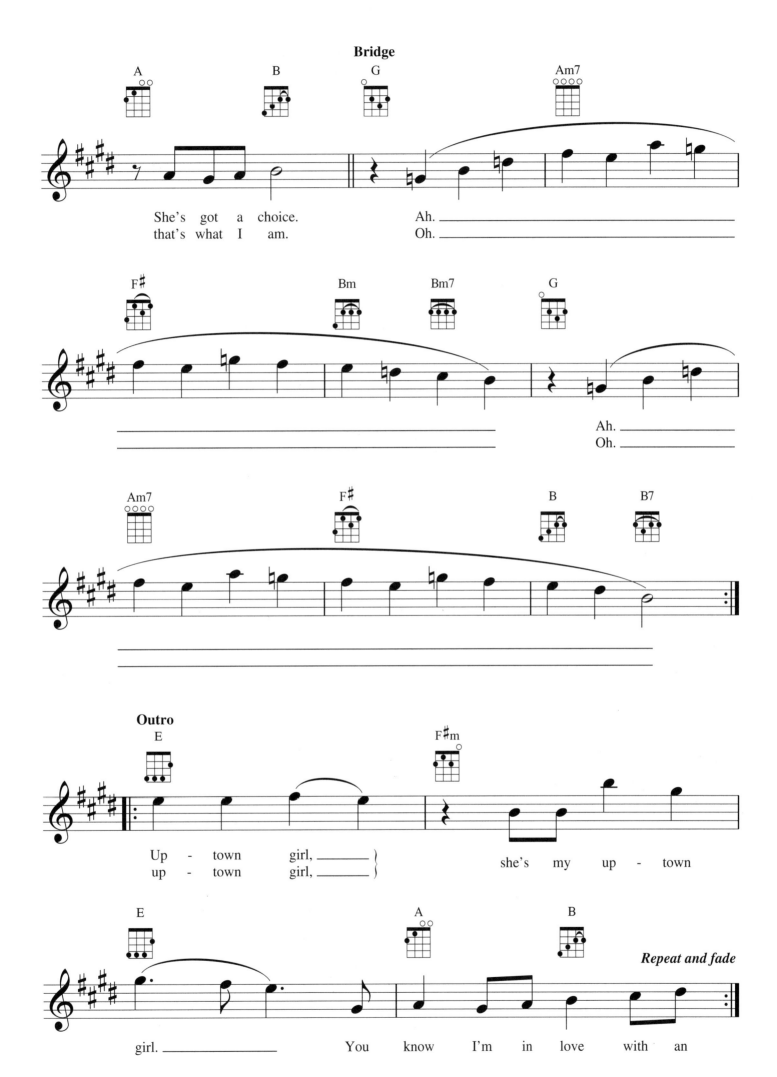

We Didn't Start the Fire

Words and Music by Billy Joel

First note

Verse
Bright Rock

1. Har - ry Tru - man, Dor - is Day, Red Chi - na, John - nie Ray,

South Pa - cif - ic, Wal - ter Win - chell, Joe Di - Mag - gi - o.

Joe Mc - Car - thy, Rich - ard Nix - on, Stu - de - bak - er, tel - e - vi - sion,

North Ko - re - a, South Ko - re - a, Mar - i - lyn Mon - roe.

Verse

2. Ro - sen - bergs, H - Bomb, Sug - ar Ray, Pan - mun - jom,

5. Bud - dy Hol - ly, Ben Hur, Space Mon - key, Ma - fi - a,

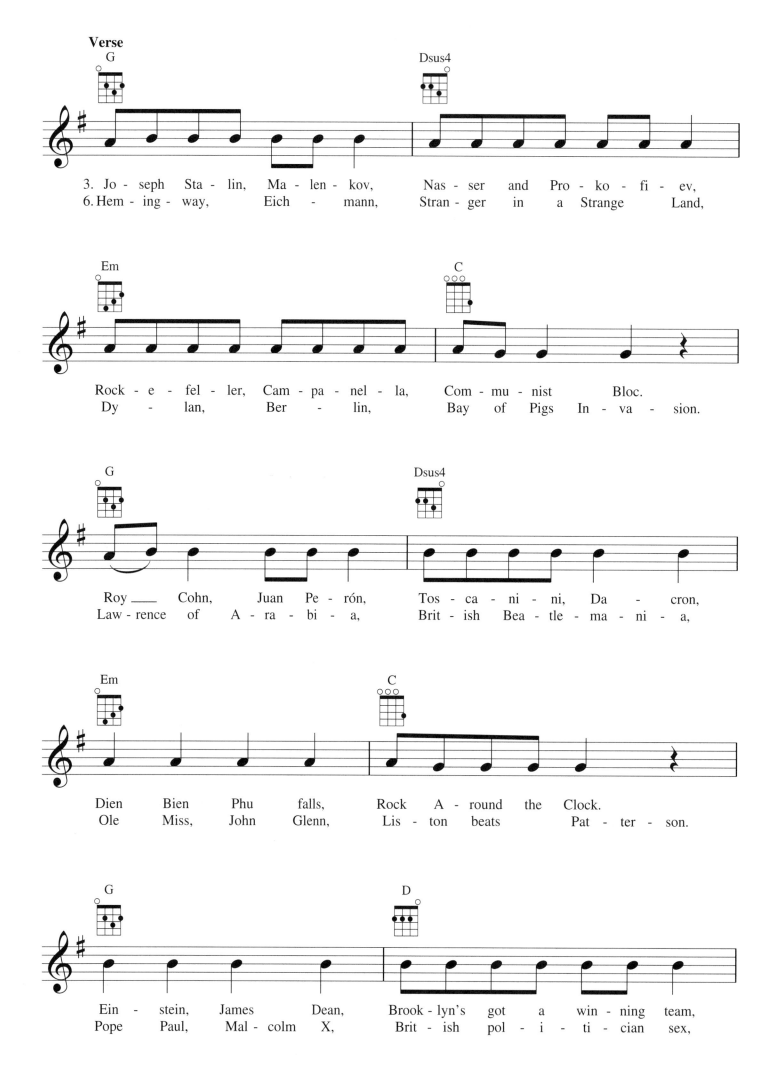

tried to fight __ it.   4. Lit - tle Rock, Pas - ter - nak,   Mic - key Man - tle, Ker - ou - ac,

Sput - nik, Chou En - Lai,   Bridge on the Riv - er Kwai.   Leb - a - non, Charles de Gaulle,

Cal - i - for - nia base - ball,   Stark- weath - er, Ho - mi - cide,   chil - dren of Tha - li - do - mide.

what else do I have to say?   We did - n't start the fi -

- re.   It was al - ways burn - ing since the world's been turn - ing.

We did-n't start the fi - re. No, we did-n't light __ it, but we

Verse

tried to fight __ it. 7. Birth con-trol, Ho Chi Minh, Rich-ard Nix-on back a-gain.

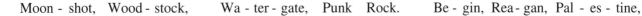

Moon - shot, Wood - stock, Wa - ter - gate, Punk Rock. Be - gin, Rea - gan, Pal - es - tine,

Ter - ror on the air - line, ay - a - tol - lahs in I - ran, Rus - sians in Af - ghan - i - stan.

Wheel of For - tune, Sal - ly Ride, Heav - y Met - al, Su - i - cide, For - eign debts, Home - less vets,

Outro-Chorus

AIDS, Crack, Ber-nie Goetz. Hy-po-der-mics on the shore, Chi-na's un-der mar-tial law,

Rock and Roll-er, Co-la Wars, I can't take it an-y-more. We did-n't start the fi-

-re. It was al-ways burn - ing since the world's been turn - ing.

We did-n't start the fi - re. But when we are gone, __ will it

still burn on, ___ and on, _____ and on, ___ and on, _____ and on, ___ and on, __

____ and on, ___ and on? _____